MEET THE KEY WORKERS

FOOD SERVICE
WORKERS

BY
SHALINI VALLEPUR

KidHaven
PUBLISHING

Published in 2024 by
KidHaven Publishing, an Imprint of Greenhaven Publishing, LLC
2544 Clinton St., Buffalo, NY 14224

© 2022 Booklife Publishing
This edition is published by arrangement with Booklife Publishing

Written by: Shalini Vallepur
Edited by: John Wood
Designed by: Jasmine Pointer

Cataloging-in-Publication Data

Names: Vallepur, Shalini.
Title: Food service workers / Shalini Vallepur.
Description: New York : KidHaven Publishing, 2024. | Series: Meet the key workers | Includes glossary and index.
Identifiers: ISBN 9781534544482 (pbk) | ISBN 9781534544499 (library bound) | ISBN 9781534544505 (ebook)
Subjects: LCSH: Food service-- Juvenile literature | Occupation-- Juvenile literature
Classification: LCC HD8039.F7 V35 2024 | DDC 331.7--dc23

All rights reserved. No part of this book may be reproduced in any form without permission in writing from the publisher, except by a reviewer.

Manufactured in the United States of America

CPSIA compliance information: Batch #CSKH24: For further information contact Greenhaven Publishing LLC at 1-844-317-7404.

Please visit our website, www.greenhavenpublishing.com. For a free color catalog of all our high-quality books, call toll free 1-844-317-7404 or fax 1-844-317-7405.

Find us on

Image Credits

All images are courtesy of Shutterstock.com, unless otherwise specified. With thanks to Getty Images, Thinkstock Photo and iStockphoto.

Cover – kurhan, Studio Romantic, melhijad, Vector_dream_team, Inspiring, Magnia, HappyPictures, Masa Marinkovic. 2–3 – Iakov Filimonov. 4–5 – VAKS-Stock Agency, vichie81. 6–7 – Olena Yakobchuk, Slatan, Budimir Jevtic, Inspiring. 8–9 – jongcreative, Tukaram.Karve, alicja neumiler, chung toan co, Radu Cadar. 10–11 – JP WALLET, HappyPictures, Monkey Business Images, Kwame Amo, Pogorelova Olga, maradaisy. 12–13 – Avigator Fortuner, Aleksandar Malivuk, Jarek Kilian. 14–15 – Inspiring, Dmitry Kalinovsky, SeventyFour, jc.space, 279photo Studio, Top Vector Studio, uiliaaa. 16–17 – robuart, gpointstudio, Kzenon, Iakov Filimonov. 18–19 – Pressmaster, Dmitry Kalinovsky, StockSmartStart, Pro Symbols. 20–21 – HASPhotos, Monkey Business Images, elenabsl, Gurza. 22–23 – Diego Cervo, CharacterFamily70.

CONTENTS

Page 4 — Here to Help

Page 6 — People in Food

Page 8 — On the Farm

Page 12 — On the Way

Page 14 — In the Factory

Page 16 — At the Supermarket

Page 20 — Food Banks

Page 22 — Food for Thought

Page 24 — Glossary and Index

Words that look like **this** can be found in the glossary on page 24.

HERE TO HELP

There are lots of jobs in the world and each one is different. Some jobs are always needed. The people who do these jobs are called key workers.

Key can sometimes mean needed and important.

Firefighters are always needed in case there is a fire.

Firefighter

Without key workers, we would not have the things we need to live safely, such as food and important **services**.

5

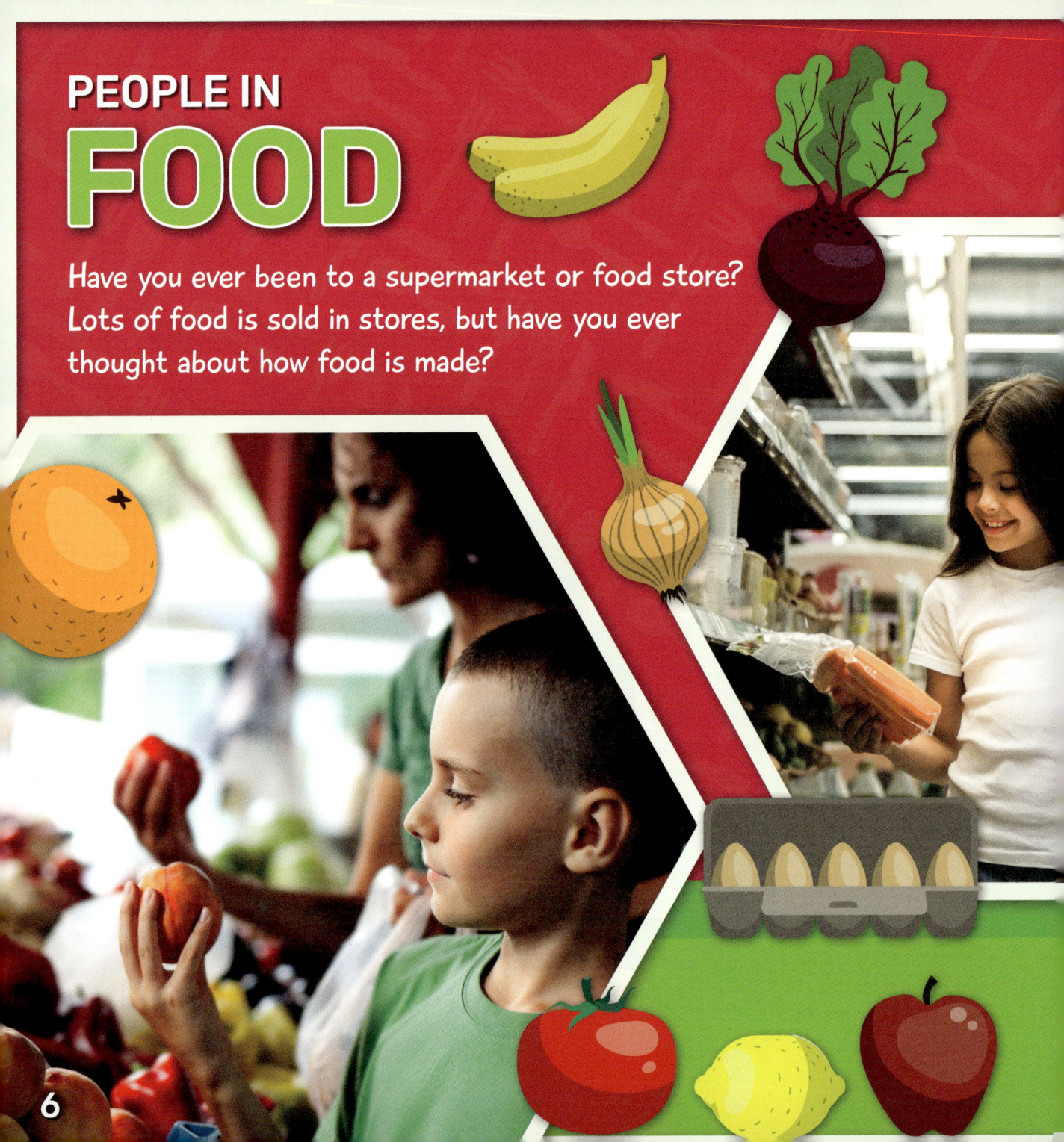

PEOPLE IN FOOD

Have you ever been to a supermarket or food store? Lots of food is sold in stores, but have you ever thought about how food is made?

Who grows the food? And who makes sure that food gets to the stores? Lots of people work to make sure we have food. Let's learn all about them!

7

ON THE FARM

Most of the food that we buy starts off on farms. Farmers work hard all year round to grow **crops**. They plant the crops and care for them as they grow.

When the crops are ready for **harvest**, they are picked by farm workers and pickers. Crops may be picked by hand.

Working on a farm is tough!

Some farms use big machines, such as tractors, to harvest and carry crops. The farmers need special skills to use these machines.

Some farmers raise farm animals. If an animal is sick, the farmer may call a **vet**. Vets give **medicine** to sick animals and make sure they are well.

ON THE WAY

After being harvested, crops are usually taken to factories. Workers put the crops onto trucks or trains and they are taken to a factory.

Container ship

We get food from all over the world thanks to people working on container ships.

Sometimes crops are shipped around the world. Workers pack and put the crops onto airplanes or big container ships.

13

IN THE FACTORY

Crops are brought to factories where they are **processed** into lots of different foods and packaged. Factory workers check the foods and make sure that the factory machines are working properly.

Drivers use forklifts to carry food around the factory. When the food is ready to be sold, drivers load it onto trucks. Then, the trucks take the food to stores and supermarkets.

Crops can be turned into all sorts of foods!

15

AT THE SUPERMARKET

Lots of people work in supermarkets and they are there to help! Supermarket assistants put food onto the shelves when it arrives.

Bakers and butchers work at some supermarkets. They know all about the food they serve and help us get the exact food we want.

When we are ready to pay for the food, we go to the cashier. The cashier adds up the cost of everything.

Supermarkets must be clean because there is a lot of food! Cleaners work hard to make sure everything is clean and tidy.

FOOD BANKS

A food bank is like a supermarket, but the food does not cost anything. Food banks get their food from **donations**.

Sometimes, people may not have enough to eat. A food bank can really help them.

Why not check if there are any food banks in your area that you can donate to?

Most food banks are run by volunteers. Being a volunteer means you do not get paid for the work you do. Volunteers work really hard to make sure people have enough to eat.

FOOD FOR THOUGHT

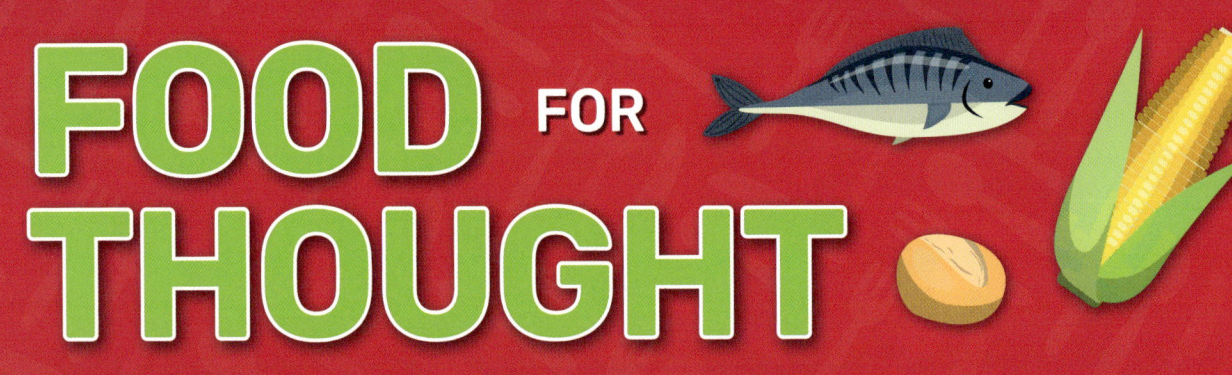

Lots of people work extremely hard to make sure we have food. The next time you eat something, think about where it came from and who helped to get it to the store.

Always say thank you to the people who help!

22

Now you know about the people who work in food! Can you match each job below to the right person?

Farmer	Truck driver	Supermarket assistant
Grows crops to eat	Drives crops to factories	Puts food on supermarket shelves

GLOSSARY

crops	plants that are grown on a farm
donations	things that have been given away for a cause such as a charity
harvest	when fully grown plants or crops are picked
medicine	something used or taken to fight off diseases
processed	changed or made into something else
services	tasks or actions that people pay other people to do, such as caring for older people, fixing things that are broken, or cleaning
vet	a doctor who is trained to take care of animals

INDEX

airplanes 13
animals 11
crops 8–10, 12–15, 23
factories 12, 14–15, 23
farms 8–11, 23
ships 13
supermarkets 6, 15–17, 19–20, 23
tractors 10
trucks 12, 15, 23
vets 11
volunteers 21